LOVING
THOSE
WE'D
RATHER
HATE

*DEVELOPING COMPASSION
IN AN ANGRY WORLD*

LOVING THOSE WE'D RATHER HATE

JOSEPH M. STOWELL

MOODY PRESS

CHICAGO

*"If the foundations are destroyed,
what can the righteous do?"*

(Psalm 11:3)

John Paulk will never forget the 1986 Gay Pride parade in downtown Columbus, Ohio. As a well-known female impersonator, he was riding in the back of a red Mustang convertible dressed in a white linen suit and a blonde wig.

"Candi, we love you!" a man yelled. "You're the most gorgeous drag queen in Columbus!" John smiled and waved.

As the motorcade progressed, John heard taunts and jeers coming from a small crowd of people waving Bibles over their heads, holding signs that read, "God Hates Fags" and "Turn or Burn."[1]

In Pensacola, Florida, an abortion protest took a radical turn as Michael Griffin pulled a gun and murdered the doctor who ran the abortion clinic. A similar incident occurred several months later in Wichita, Kansas, where an abortion clinic doctor was shot and wounded. While we would have expected a raised voice of outrage from pro-life leaders, several, while reflecting regret for the event,

5

modified the commentary by rationalizing the killing in terms of losing one life to save many unborn lives.

Granted, most of us would not have been in that Bible-waving, taunting crowd at the gay rights parade, nor would we think for a moment to justify killing anyone, whether born or unborn. But a lot of us, if honest with ourselves, find that hostile and negative feelings are close to the surface these days. Listen to how we discuss political and cultural issues with each other and what we mutter under our breath when we watch the evening news. I don't know that there has ever been a time in modern church history when Christians have been angry about more things than we seem to be now.

We're mad about movies, the media, and militant movements that radicalize the causes of women, gays, and lesbians. We're mad about the ACLU, condoms in the school, crime on the street, and drugs in our neighborhoods. We're mad about education, the impact of society on our children, and abortion activists.

Perhaps our anger is rooted in the fact that our society has become so offensive to us. We're offended by the blatant sexuality of advertising, by the fact that Christians are mocked in sitcoms and movies. We're offended that no one really values our point of view or what we have to say even when our most articulate spokesmen speak the truth in reasoned and rational ways. Perhaps we're offended by the fact that groups that never were a part of the fabric of this great nation through all the years of its birth, growth, maturity, and success have now come along and gained a power place in the culture, advancing hostile agendas that threaten our peace and security.

We're offended that from the White House to local politicians, those who represent agendas contrary to the founding principles of this culture have more say and influence than those of us who represent the heritage of the land. Perhaps we're upset because we are now behind the power curve in this culture and have become underclassed in a land whose values used to affirm what we believed, in a land where we used to be able to trust that school teachers, politicians, and cultural heroes would uphold the values that we worked so hard to teach our children.

It was interesting to sense the pulse of the church the day after November 3, 1992. That was the election day when candidates from the White House to the Senate to state and local posts were swept into office as a result of a campaign that discounted the themes of moral and family values and promised to put impetus behind the advance of gays and abortionists. Something dramatic had happened, and we felt its impact. Since the late seventies, we as Christians had had our say in government and, in fact, had been largely influential in placing presidents in Washington, D.C. They entertained us, and they often were willing to put the power of their office behind issues that we felt were vitally important to our nation. Our place was so potent that the cover of *Newsweek* magazine declared 1976 "The Year of the Evangelicals."[2] It was obvious, however, that by 1992 the sun had set on us. In that election year, the political power brokers and press ignored us and more often than not distorted our views and chided us for being bigoted, intolerant, and out-of-step with a progressive America.

Our distinct feeling was that God had lost on that November third. Actually, nothing could be further from the truth. God didn't lose, and the church was not defeated. It was Christ who said, "I will build My church, and the gates of hell shall not prevail against it" (Matthew 16:18). His finished work on the cross has already guaranteed that ultimately Christ will put all of the enemies of God away (1 Corinthians 15:24–25). The day will come when at the name of Jesus every knee shall bow and every tongue will confess that Jesus Christ is Lord to the glory of the Father (Philippians 2:9–11). In fact, Romans 13 teaches us that <u>God places rulers in authority and takes them down</u>. For some reason best known to Him, His sovereign permission has granted this element of our society its day in the sun.

<u>What we know to be true about God is that He uses even the worst things that He permits to come to His ultimate praise</u>, gain, and glory. His long-range perspectives transcend the daily dealings in the corridors within the beltway of Washington, D.C. His plan is a macro movement, managed by <u>His sovereign purposes, over which He has full and unchallenged control.</u>

Yet somehow we had forgotten these truths. And our despair on that day matured through the months that followed into a sense of defeat that has us by the heart. That sense of defeat has given rise to a church that presents itself in this political environment as cynical, disrespectful, intimidated, insecure, angry, and often irrational. We shout cruel and demeaning taunts at gay activists, shoot at abortionists, spread rumors about and speak disrespectfully of authorities God has placed in our lives.

Are We Missing Something?

Bill Hybels, pastor of Willow Creek Community Church in Barrington, Illinois, has struck up a friendship with President Bill Clinton that has taken some unusual turns. On a recent visit to Chicago, the president called Bill and asked to have breakfast with him. Bill has been to the White House to meet with the president and has been entertained in the Lincoln Room as an overnight guest. Bill's desire is to affect Mr. Clinton in terms of the president's relationship to Christ and sensitivity to the moral issues that we all care about. Bill values the friendship as an important bridge over which God's truths can be carried into the arena of the president's heart. What has proven to be interesting and somewhat surprising is that Bill has come under intense criticism for being a friend of the president. And in fact, some have threatened to cut off major financial support for his ministry.

While we would all have differing opinions about Bill Clinton as president of the United States, I would trust that all of us in the body of Christ would sense a deep compulsion to care about him as a person and about his relationship to Jesus Christ. But somehow it seems that our consternation has eclipsed the sense of compassion that makes our Christianity so compellingly unique in a cruel and unforgiving world.

The world doesn't miss the point. For the most part they see us now as just another political action group that's upset about having its rights trampled and its point of view marginalized. Unfortunately, we have given the world reason to discount us as some of our high-profile leaders fail morally, others discredit the faith through greedy schemes of gain, and in large numbers we take to the streets demanding that the culture respect our views, mounting our soapboxes and insisting that political systems conform to biblical principles.

Granted, from our side of the fence it's easy to understand the rising temperatures in the body of Christ. To know God and to seek to be like God means that we affirm righteousness and feel the offense of unrighteousness, especially when it's so blatant. If our hearts and minds didn't tilt as we observed the decadence of our world, there would be something wrong with our Christianity. So we're not dysfunctional when it comes to an inner outrage over injustice and sin. Our letters to the editors, our heated conversations with one another, and the almost fanatical allegiance some of us have to spokesmen like Rush Limbaugh are, in one sense, a sign that our spiritual and moral sensitivities are grieved by the great loss we have witnessed in our country.

At the same time, we have to ask ourselves if a vitally important quality isn't missing in the expression of our Christianity. Whatever happened to a church marked by mercy, compassion, grace, and a willingness to suffer if necessary for the cause of Christ, while in the midst of it all maintaining a posture of love for and forgiveness toward our enemies (1 Peter 2:19–25)? Was it not to a wicked and spiritually misdirected culture that Christ, as He hung on the cross being rejected and tortured, said, "Father, forgive them . . ."? Do we as Christians really just want to be another group that is mad about its loss of power and influence and its place in society being undervalued? Do we really want to be just another political minority, another protest in the streets; or is there something more dramatically unique and powerful that has gotten lost in the struggle?

I think so!

Choosing Issues Carefully

It should not go unnoticed that both Jesus Christ and the early church, through the first three centuries of its existence, found themselves thriving in an environment that was politically and culturally far more pagan than America is today. A close scrutiny of the ministry of Christ and the apostles displays a far different attitude in their responses and an unusual lack of rancor toward the culture. In fact, the harshest words of Christ and the apostles are not directed toward the pagan culture in which they lived, but toward the religious leaders of their day who distorted truth. It was for the Pharisees who were deceiving the people and the temple salesmen who were ripping off the pilgrims by overcharging them for sacrificial animals that Christ reserved His strongest condemnation. Heresy and greed at the expense of God's people were, in Christ's perspective, intolerable. The theme runs through the rest of the New Testament as well, as the apostles speak most strongly about those who pose as religious and spiritual leaders but then deceive and disadvantage innocent followers (2 Timothy 3:1–9).

It's interesting to note that we seem to have a disconcerting tolerance for those who, while claiming the name of Christ, mislead people regarding the truth of Christ, often for their own gain and glory. In fact, the dramatic shift in our culture has created some liaisons with other religionists who hold our sense of moral concern. And although there is something to be said for doing everything we can to peacefully and graciously hold our culture and our politicians accountable for righteousness and to join forces with others who will lend power to the project, we must always be reminded that this does not make us spiritual colleagues with those who deny orthodoxy in the ongoing work of the kingdom. At times it appears we have it backward, denouncing with great intensity the paganism of our day while embracing without differentiation political partners who, in both preaching and practice, distort and often deny the truth of the kingdom.

The focus of both Christ and the church toward the pagan environment was not just a focus on the politics, decadent lifestyles, and influences of the day. It was a focus that went deeper than that. It went beyond that which is temporal and distasteful to that which is eternal. To them the compelling priority was people who were lost, regardless of political or lifestyle issues; people who, not surprisingly, were simply living out the fallenness that they had inherited from birth. In fact, the heartthrob of both Christ and the early church was a clear sense of compassion toward those who were lost. Wasn't it our

Lord who said that He had come to seek and to save that which was lost (Luke 19:10)?

By What Are We Known?

I fear that looking at some of us within the church of Christ today, it would be hard to see that we are on a seek-and-save mission since we look so much more like we're into search-and-destroy. I have to wonder if the doctor who heads the abortion clinic in our neighborhood would say that one thing he knows for sure is that "these Christians are adamantly against what I do, but they seem to have an unusual concern for me as a person." Wouldn't it be a shock if a pastor of a local church were to call the doctor of the local abortion clinic and ask him to lunch? And during the course of that time together communicate his clear objection to the doctor's practice, yet let him know that he cared about him as a person, about his family, and more than that, about the realities of his relationship to eternity?

I have a sneaking suspicion that in many churches in America, if the pastor were to get up on Sunday morning and say, "This coming Saturday we're going to marshal our forces to go to the local abortion clinic and protest the death of innocent lives and seek to save as many babies as possible"—especially if he offered a nice pancake-and-eggs breakfast at 8:30—chances are he'd get a pretty decent crowd for the day. If on the next Sunday he got up and said that this coming Saturday the church had planned another strategic kingdom event—based on the fact that they live in a community full of people who have been born but who are dead in trespasses and sin and are liable for the eternal judgment of God—and then announced that there would be another great pancake breakfast at 8:30, a time of training, and a blitzing of the community on behalf of reaching those whose eternities were in peril, my guess is that there would be a lot fewer out the second Saturday than there were the first. The reality that there wouldn't be nearly the fervor for the second Saturday is a reflection that we as a church have yet to be consumed with the focus of the ministry of Christ and the early church.

In fact, we need to consider the possibility that posturing ourselves so forthrightly in terms of political concerns may even be a barrier to our capacity to reach those who are on the other side of the political fence from us, since we have formed alliances against them and have presented ourselves as their enemies.

As elections and campaigns heat

up, it is not uncommon to see church lobbies filled with literature delineating the right candidates to vote for and marshaling the flock to put people in power who will defend and promote the values that we hold to be important. Although pastors need to clearly delineate righteous perspectives on cultural values and every Christian certainly should exercise the right as a citizen to hold our leaders morally accountable at the ballot box, I do find myself wondering what would happen if a candidate on the other side, his campaign manager, family, friends, or supporters would walk into our church and see that his opponent is being promoted. I wonder if there would be an immediate barrier built against the ministry of the Cross in their lives. It's not that an election is unimportant, it's that sometimes we have to measure what is more strategically important. Christ clearly taught us that the priority of a person's soul was of utmost significance.

Does the church really want to posture itself as being long on politics and short on the potential of penetrating all who live around us with the liberating gospel of Christ? Do we really want to look as though we are long on mad and short on mercy? That we are more full of consternation than we are of compassion? I

17

think we have to remember that it's not a matter of whether or not we have legitimate cause to be concerned and to feel a measure of righteous anger about what's happening around us. It's a matter, rather, of what finally and ultimately is most important. As the church, we have to choose our issues carefully and make sure that lesser issues do not obstruct progress and advance in terms of greater issues.

On a recent trip to England I noticed an unusual thing about their tow trucks. I have always known them as "wreckers." But the ones I saw in England have the word "Recovery" written on them. Same instrument, same mission, but a radically different perspective.

God has called us to missions of recovery in terms of persons who need a Savior.

Recovery

John Paulk used to ride in the back of red Mustangs flaunting himself as the drag queen in Columbus, but he no longer rides in those parades because he has come to know Jesus Christ as his personal Savior. Today John and his wife Anne live in Portland, Oregon, where he is pursuing college studies in preparation for a professional career in Christian counseling. Though John still occasionally struggles with temptations and memories of the lifestyle he left, with the help of God and his Christian community he is well on his way to wholeness. Soon after his repentant conversion to Christ, John moved to California to become part of Love In Action, a ministry of The Church of the Open Door. He relates, "Heterosexual men befriended me, prayed for me, and invited me into their homes for fellowship. They treated me with genuine respect and affection. It's really that simple. They loved me into wholeness."

What is instructive is that John found Jesus Christ through a local pastor. Six months after John rode in that parade, this pastor befriended John at the print shop where he worked and one day invited himself over to John's apartment. Although John suspected the minister was coming to talk about God, he consented. That night, they prayed together as John committed his life to Christ.

Courage, Compassion, and Clout

Too many times, as Christians we allow an offense from an individual or an organization's moral stand to keep us from a caring involvement in their lives. Imagine, however, how offended Christ must have been, being the holy God used to the culture and context of the glory of heaven, to have the culture around Him change dramatically as He came into a world so full of gross and decadent sin. If anyone would have had the right to rally the world to a revolution against pagan powers and imperialistic politics, it would have been Christ. In fact, He could have massed angelic forces to lead the charge. And whereas none of us would ever say that He didn't feel the offense of the sin around Him, we would also have to admit that the overriding priority—the primary focus of His intense three years of ministry and the culmination of His unparalleled sacrifice on the Cross— was reaching those who were hopelessly and helplessly separated from His Father. He came to restore them to a redemptive relationship, to fit them for life here and in the world to come. Since that was the posture of Christ, must we not measure our posture and priorities by that standard as well?

Both the apostles and the ensuing generations in the early church maintained the same focus. It was obviously not their primary purpose to change their political or cultural environment, but rather to faithfully purify their own lives and let the resultant light of their good works shine through them, which in turn would begin to have a healing influence on the culture. Their strategy did not focus on political posturing, but on the undeniably powerful change that comes when people are redeemed, filled with the Spirit, and leading obedient lives that generate compelling outcomes in their own character, homes, churches, and communities. For three hundred years Christians were fed to lions to entertain the crowds and covered with pitch, tied to lamp posts, and set on fire to light the streets of Rome. Yet they remained faithful to the agenda of an unintimidated allegiance to Jesus Christ. Soon the power that came through their authentically valiant and courageous adherence to their Master became so powerful that Constantine, the emperor of the great Roman political system, declared that he could no longer fight against it and named Christianity as the official religion of the empire.

Through it all, the church remained in a compassionate posture toward the people who ignored and often oppressed them.

Nothing is perhaps more dramatically instructive to us in trying to put into balance the decadence of our day and our dedication to the spirit of authentic Christianity than the setting in Luke 15 where Jesus Christ told the story of the prodigal son. In fact, Luke 15 houses three of Christ's most familiar stories. The stories of the lost sheep and the lost coin, as well as the lost son, find their place in the context of this chapter. What is common to all three of these stories is that something of value and worth has been lost.

Lost Valuables

You may know that in the day that Christ told these stories, sheep were the measure of a person's wealth. People didn't have portfolios of stocks and bonds, but rather their wealth was in their land and their flocks. So He tells the story of what would be seen as a relatively poor shepherd who only had 100 sheep. One of them was lost. That was a significant blow, since his flock was of great value to Him. Christ said that the shepherd did what any shepherd would instinctively do, that is, go after the lamb until it was found.

The second story is of a widow who had a bag of coins, her social security fund. She lost one of the coins. She, too, had obviously lost something of value that was worthy to be pursued.

And what shall we say of a father who loses a son?

We need to remind ourselves that Christ never told stories to entertain the crowd. He told stories on purpose, with a purpose. As with all His parables, these stories make a profound point. And the point is that God has suffered a significant loss in terms of individuals whom He created in His image for the purpose of relationship, fellowship, and glory. His response is thus to pursue those who are unalterably and hopelessly separated from Him in sin, guilty before Him, and liable for eternal judgment. It is instructive that He doesn't view these lost ones as enemies to be despised and annihilated, but rather as persons of value and worth to be reclaimed.

That this is the point of these stories is clear, as the chapter opens with Christ ministering to a crowd of "tax-gathers and sinners" huddled around Him and listening intently to His teaching. These, as you may know, were the worst kind of people the Jews knew. Tax collectors sold themselves to the occupying pagan empire to collect the exorbitant taxes of Rome and then added additional assessments to line their own pockets. What could be more distasteful to an Israelite whose allegiance was to God and whose daily embarrassment was that his proud nation had become subject to the pagan and decadent empire of Rome? And then there were the "sinners"—those Jews who, though sharing in the ethnic heritage of the people of God, had no interest in or allegiance to the laws of God by which Jews lived their lives.

Two critically important elements rise to the surface in these first two verses. First, Christ was obviously interested in the lives of these worst kind of people of His day. Second, what adds real drama to the context is that the religious people of Christ's day were standing around the fringe of the crowd grumbling and complaining that Christ was spending time with people like this. To the Pharisees, these people had so violated their sense of political loyalty and religious propriety that they couldn't tolerate the fact that Christ was not castigating them but was rather compassionately reaching out to them. In the Pharisees' minds, if Christ was really who He claimed to be, God in the flesh, then He would be standing with them at the fringe of the crowd heartily condemning people like this.

God's Loss

It was into this context that Christ told these three stories to make one penetrating point: God has suffered a significant loss, He cares for what He has lost, and He will go to great lengths to reclaim them for eternity. It is instructive to note that Christ's interests clearly went beyond the politics, practices, and perceptions of the temporal realities of His day to the penetrating and profound ramifications of eternal destinies.

And so He told the story of the shepherd. If you were the shepherd, wouldn't you spend your time going after that which was lost? And if you were a widow, wouldn't you find it to be a pressing priority to recover that which you have lost?

To emphasize His point of God's compassionate addiction to the lost, Christ dramatically shifts the scene from what would have been normally acceptable persons like shepherds and widows to a story about a young man whose life was an offense to basic religious and societal values, a reprehensible example of a lifestyle gone wrong.

In the story, the prodigal represents the "tax-gatherers and sinners" to whom Christ is extending His compassion in verses one and two. The father of the prodigal represents God the Father. The elder brother, who complains bitterly about the father's compassionate and forgiving attention to such an undeserving, offensive person, represents the religious ones of Christ's day who stood around the fringe of the crowd grumbling, saying, "This man receives sinners and eats with them."

The story of the prodigal son is a story about a person whom most people in the days of Jesus Christ would have flat out rejected and never felt a moment's guilt. Christ sketched the story of the prodigal whose offenses were two-fold. First, he blatantly offended the most treasured and revered values of society; second, as a result, he became offensive as an individual in terms of his decadent lifestyle and resultant degraded condition.

Unthinkable Offenses

In one sense, you probably had to be a Jew living in those days to understand the impact of the story. An understanding of the Jewish culture makes it clear how very offensive Christ wished to paint this boy's behavior. In verse 12 we read, "The younger of them said to his father, 'Father, give me the share of the estate that falls to me.'" Even today in the Palestinian culture if a person asks his parents for the estate ahead of time, it's like saying to his parents, "I wish you were dead." It is simply never done. It is the depth of disrespect toward family and parentage. The Pharisees listening to this story would have immediately recoiled at the thought and felt the impact of his actions against that father.

The second offense unfolds in the following verse, "And not many days later, the younger son gathered everything together and went on a journey into a distant country." *Gathering everything together* literally means that he cashed out his portion of the estate. This was the second rejection of basic cultural values perpetrated by this boy on his father and family. In order for this boy to take cash to the distant country, he had to sell his portion of the estate, which would have meant selling family property. Again, even a reflection on modern Palestinian culture informs us that land is part and parcel of family heritage and legacy. People rarely, and only in extreme circumstances, sell family land in the East. In fact, if you know anything about the political struggle over the West Bank territory in Israel, you're aware that the Palestinians claim the land as their national legacy by divine right. And so do the Jews. That's why it's so difficult to reach a compromise in terms of dividing the land, because the land is more than their possession; it's their heritage.

A graphic story from the Old Testament illustrates this societal value when King Ahab, who didn't have an herb garden, called in Naboth whose family land adjoined the king's property. Ahab pleaded with Naboth to sell him a portion of his vineyard so that the king might have property for an herb garden. Needless to say, it would be somewhat appealing to be called into the king's presence and to be offered a portion of the king's wealth for a piece of property that you held. Most of us would have sold it in a minute. The price would have been right, and the honor of doing business with the king would no doubt have been compelling. For us, real estate is simply a place to live. We are like tumbleweeds, buying and selling property to our own advantage, rarely thinking about its intrinsic value to our own personal history. Not so in the Jewish culture.

According to 1 Kings, "Ahab spoke to Naboth, saying, 'Give me your vineyard, that I may have it for a vegetable garden because it is close beside my house, and I will give you a better vineyard than it in its place; if you like, I will give you the price of it in money.' But Naboth said to Ahab, 'The Lord forbid me that I should give you the inheritance of my fathers'" (21:2–3). What unfolds from that point on is a sad story of a plot spun by Jezebel, the king's wife, to call false witnesses against Naboth so that his life can be taken unjustly, leaving the king free to assume ownership of the sought after land. So vile a sin was this in the sight of God that He summoned the prophet Elijah to go and speak to Ahab. Elijah found Ahab roaming through his newly acquired property and pronounced God's judgment on him, predicting that as the dogs licked Naboth's blood in the streets, so the day would come that Ahab's blood would flow in the streets as well for the dogs to lick (1 Kings 21:17–24).

It should not be surprising, then, that the prodigal son would have gone to a distant country, because there was no way that a boy doing what this boy had done to offend such fundamental family values could have stayed in his hometown.

When he went to the far country, he spent the estate in loose living. The squandering of the family assets was more than just a waste of money. He had depleted a significant portion of the family's social security fund. In that day, there was no social security system, but rather the elderly of the family were cared for by the revenue stream created by the land and flock holdings on the estate. This boy had deflated the family's capacity to care for their aging parents by not only selling the assets but also wasting them on a wanton lifestyle—an offense that would not have been missed by the Pharisees who were now attentively monitoring the repugnant details of the parable Christ was unfolding.

Not only had this boy committed these deep offenses, but as a result of his rebellious choices he had become a person so degraded that both his lifestyle and his person were reprehensible to any decent Jew.

Christ characterizes him as having spent all his resources, leaving him empty, helpless, and hopeless in the face of a severe famine that has come. Most decent, hard-working, law-abiding Jews would have been tempted at this point to turn their backs and, while walking away, mutter something like, "He made his bed; let him lie in it," or, perhaps, "Why should I feel sorry for him? What about his family that he's hurt so deeply?"

In his spent and hopeless condition, he found that his life had been reduced to *shame.* He attached himself in servitude to a Gentile and was given the assignment of keeping the pigs. Most of us would ask, "What's a nice Jewish boy like you doing in a place like this?" But beyond that, to someone aligned with Judaism, the defilement of this boy's shame was extreme given the fact that he was living twenty-four hours a day in an environment ceremonially and spiritually unclean.

Beyond the shame lay the inevitable *sorrow* as he sought to fill his stomach with the pods fed to the pigs but remained empty and malnourished. In the Eastern culture, there are two kinds of carob pods. One is rich in nutrients. In fact, there is an ancient proverb that says if a child has a pocketful of carob pods he is a fortunate child. There is another kind of carob pod, however, that is simply fibrous in its content. This is the kind that grows on scrubby bushes that is fed to the pigs. It was all he had to eat and it did not satisfy.

The sorrow in this spent, shameful life was deep. And the despair sent him on a search for something to hope in, for someone to help him. With all of his options expired, he became aware that his only hope would be in the fact that perhaps his father would forgive him and accept him back as a servant.

It is clear that Christ is seeking to make a point: For the worst kind of people in this world, there is a source of hope in rectifying the spentness, shame, and sorrow of their lives, and that is in the mercy of a forgiving father.

And so the boy rose and began his long journey home, no doubt along the same road he had walked some months before, when he had been so full of hope, dreams, and resources, unknowing that his rebellious, self-serving, self-sufficient pattern of life would leave him in shambles.

The Worth of the Sinner

At this point Christ takes the story through a dramatic set of turns that both shock and reprove the uncompassionate, disassociated hearts of the religious folks standing around the edge of the crowd.

As the boy makes his way home, the text says that "while he was still a long way off, his father saw him, and felt compassion for him . . ." I can't help but wonder, knowing what I do about God the Father, if Christ wasn't indicating here that this father had often gazed down that path wondering, hoping, waiting for the day that his son would come home. It is true that God stands, before ultimate judgment is necessary, in a compassionate posture, ready and willing to receive the repentant sinner to Himself, the only source of hope and healing.

Not only does it appear that the father is waiting for the son, but when he sees the son coming he takes the initiative and runs to meet him, throws his arms around him, and kisses him over and over again, which is a sign in the Jewish culture for receptivity and welcome. He embraces the boy who is clothed with his torn and tattered garments, defiled by that which is spiritually unclean and reprehensible to the Jews. And he does it publicly. Perhaps even by the city gate, in front of the elders who sat there. This is something that no Jewish father would have ever done and that no upstanding Jew of that day would have believed would happen. The boy deserves nothing but justice and punishment, and instead he finds in his father compassion and grace. In fact, the boy is so stunned by his father's grace that he breaks in repentance before his father and says, "Father, I have sinned against heaven and in your sight; I am no longer worthy to be called your son." It is important to note that when he was in a far land he had practiced his speech, and as recorded in verse 19, he added to his speech the closing line, "Make me as one of your hired men." In the best of manuscripts this is not repeated when he comes face-to-face with the compassion and grace of his dad.

Hired men were the most independent of all the servants who worked on an estate. The bond slaves were the most deeply indebted slaves who had committed the rest of their lives out of love and gratitude to the master for his goodness to them. The truly repentant response on the boy's part would have been to offer himself as a bond slave. Household servants were one step above the bond slaves in terms of position and stature. And then there were the hired men. These were day laborers who lived in the village and came to the estate to do a day's work, took their paycheck, and went home. This was the most independent of all the workers. Actually, the boy in his shame and sorrow wanted to cut a deal with his dad and, while reflecting repentance, maintain a measure of independence. It was not true repentance, just an attempt at self-reformation. Yet the amazing grace of his father changed all that. It caused the boy's heart to melt and to throw himself on the full mercy of his father.

What makes the story even more dramatic is the fact that Christ went on to say that the father did not put the boy on probation to see if he was truly sorry and whether he had changed his ways, but he fully and immediately accepted his son into the family. He called for a robe—the sign of sonship, and a ring—the sign of family authority, and shoes—the proof positive that he was no longer a slave but a free man. The father fully incorporated the son into the family.

The older brother stood steaming on the sidelines, mad about the fact that the father would be so merciful and gracious to this boy. After all, hadn't he, the elder son, been faithful all the time? And didn't this boy deserve punishment and exclusion? Christ reproved the attitude of the elder brother by reminding him that the elder son's faithfulness had guaranteed all the privileges of the estate; that his lack of gratitude toward his father was less than honorable; and that his lack of compassion and mercy for his brother who once was lost but now was found was a telling lack of divine compassion and mercy in his life.

All of this to make a very clear point. Jesus Christ wanted those who held the offensive and reprehensible elements of their society at arm's length to know that if God were here, He would look on them with compassion and seek to find them, that they might be stunned by unusual grace, repent, and find a place in the family. That's why Christ was at the core of the crowd with the worst kind of people of His day.

It's interesting to note that these tax collectors and sinners were interested in listening to Christ. Obviously today some of the more rebellious elements of our society show no interest in what we have to say. In fact, they not only distance themselves but seem to be hostile toward us in their rhetoric and responses. The issue is not whether they are seekers listening to our message of hope and healing or whether they are taunting us from a distance. Rather, the issue is whether or not we have postured ourselves and created an environment that reflects that we care, so that when they reach the end of themselves and seek a refuge of hope they will come, as these tax collectors and sinners did, and listen. Creating that environment in which grace can be shared begins with our attitudes. Those reprehensible ones who are gathered around Christ wouldn't have dreamed of spending time with the Pharisees. The religionists of Christ's day had clearly communicated that this kind of people were unwelcome and despised.

Grace—Granted and Given

Creating that environment in which grace can get busy begins with following Christ's command that we stand in a forgiving, constructive posture toward the lost, as God does. Christ calls us to this in Matthew 5:43–48:

> You have heard that it was said, "You shall love your neighbor, and hate your enemy." But I say to you, love your enemies, and pray for those who persecute you in order that you may be sons of your Father who is in heaven; for He causes His sun to rise on the evil and the good, and sends rain on the righteous and the unrighteous. For if you love those who love you, what reward have you? Do not even the tax-gatherers do the same? And if you greet your brothers only, what do you do more than others? Do not even the Gentiles do the same? Therefore you are to be perfect, as your heavenly Father is perfect.[3]

At times we can carry our forgiving compassionate posture right into arenas of need. Some churches have established ministries to AIDS patients, taking the grace of God into AIDS wards and ministering not only to the victims but to their families as well. Face to Face Ministries, a ministry here in Chicago, takes the grace of God right into gay bars. Their trained staff members wear buttons announcing their identity as Christians, and in that location they carefully and courageously communicate the message of Christ. They report that they find many in these bars who are from Christian homes and many as well who are deeply hurting and searching for answers to the pain in their lives.

We cannot miss the fact that in the story of the prodigal son, the first instinctive emotion that the father felt when he saw the son coming was a surge of compassion. Compassion is one of the core qualities of God, and redemption has restored within us the capacity to reflect His likeness through our lives. A compassionless Christianity is a contradiction to the essence of our Christianity. In fact, none of us would be in the family if God had not first met us at the gates of the city and in His mercy and abundant grace taken us in and granted us full inheritance in His family as His sons and daughters. Intriguing, isn't it, that we revel so in the mercy bestowed upon us, and yet are so soon void of it when it comes to extending it to others?

No doubt some of us are saying, "Yes, but I was never a sinner like these radically reprehensible elements of our society. The depth and degradation of their sin is far worse than anything I have ever done." Have we forgotten that our holy, transcendent God is so perfect that all and any of our sin is equally offensive to Him? The ground at the foot of the cross is level, and all of us come as sinners, pleading for His grace.

This lack of compassion from those of us who have been the recipients of His unwarranted compassion is such a critical issue that when Peter questioned the Lord in Matthew 18 about the matter of forgiveness, Christ responded by telling a story about a slave who owed his king 10,000 talents. As the text says, "But since he did not have the means to repay, his lord commanded him to be sold, along with his wife and children and all that he had, and repayment to be made." In the face of this terrible plight, the slave fell down before the king and pleaded, "Have patience with me, and I will repay you everything." Christ went on to say, "And the lord of that slave felt compassion and released him and forgave him the debt." Surprisingly, however, the slave went out and found one of his fellow slaves who owed him 100 denarii, and as the text says, "he seized him and began to choke him, saying, 'Pay back what you owe.' So his fellow slave fell down and began to entreat him, saying, 'Have patience with me and I will repay you.'" But he was unwilling to forgive as he was forgiven and threw his fellow slave in prison until he could pay back what was owed. Christ concluded the story by saying that when the king heard what this forgiven slave had done, he called the slave before him and said, "Should you not also have had mercy on your fellow slave, even as I had mercy on you?" And the story says the lord, "moved with anger, handed him over to the torturers until he should repay all that was owed him" (Matthew 18:23–34).

I can't help but wonder if maybe our Lord doesn't look at us in that same context, as we, being forgiven much, have no impulse to stand in a forgiving, compassionate posture toward those who are also in need of His compassion.

Middlemen

None of us is really exempt from this tendency to posture ourselves in compassionless anger toward our enemies. In the Old Testament, one of God's finest prophets was asked to go to Nineveh, that great city, and cry against it, for, as God said, their violence had "come up" before Him. Or, in other words, God had "had it up to here" with their sin. As you probably know, Jonah immediately rose and went to Tarshish, a city that was about as far in the opposite direction as you could get in those days. His resolve not to go to Nineveh could possibly have been because he feared what it would mean for a foreigner, a Jewish prophet, to walk into the city that was the greatest city of that day, the capital of the Assyrian Empire, and call the inhabitants to repentance as he pronounced the judgment of God upon their culture.

The Assyrians were the enemies of Israel, a constant threat. And after all, they indeed were a wickedly violent culture. When they won military victories, they beheaded their captors, stacked the heads on carts, and, as they made their way back to Nineveh, celebrated the victory by building pyramids along the road—pyramids of the heads of their decapitated enemies. They preserved the bodies of the generals and captains and then when they got back to Nineveh would flay them like deer and spread their skins on the walls of the city as trophies to their great military might. Jonah would have had great reason to be intimidated and fearful in the face of this assignment. But that was not the reason he refused to go.

As he fled to Tarshish, God would not let him bail out of the plan. After a sequence of unsettling events, God banished him to three days and three nights in a sleazy underwater hotel until he was finally willing to say yes to the Master's plan. And so he went at last and proclaimed judgment on that city, and to his surprise, they repented and God forgave them and spared their lives.

You and I would think that Jonah would have been ecstatic over this tremendous and unexpected result from his evangelistic campaign. But in chapter 4 of the book of Jonah, we find Jonah outside the city, no longer mad at the Ninevites, but rather mad at God—mad at God for compassionately forgiving his enemies. It is then that Jonah admits why it was that he did not want to go in the first place when he says, "Please Lord, was not this what I said while I was still in my own country? Therefore, in order to forestall this I fled to Tarshish, for I knew that Thou art a gracious and compassionate God, slow to anger and abundant in lovingkindness, and one who relents concerning calamity" (Jonah 4:2).

It was simple. Jonah had fled to Tarshish not because he feared the Ninevites. He fled to Tarshish because he *disliked* the Ninevites. When it came to people like the Ninevites, Jonah refused to be a middle man in a compassion transaction between the merciful God of the universe and the people Jonah despised. The rest of the book of Jonah is about God's work to convince Jonah of the propriety and priority of true compassion. In fact, the message of the book of Jonah is about the depth and extent to which God's gracious and merciful compassion will extend and how far God is willing to go to enlist His people to join with Him in compassion transactions. I can't help but wonder how many of the things that happen to me throughout the course of my life are intended by God to break my proud, self-righteous, and sometimes angry heart, that I might indeed be a man after His own heart, a man who reflects a heart of genuine compassion.

A Call to Compassion

Even a casual reading of Scripture indicates that compassion is a pressing priority (see Isaiah 58:1–11; Colossians 3:10–12). One of my all-time favorite portions of Scripture,

Micah 6, finds the Jews asking God what it really takes to please Him. They go through a litany of exaggerated and excessive expressions of sacrificial loyalty to God, and the text gives the sense that almost in desperation they throw up their hands and say, "What does it take to please You?!" We've all had people around our lives who are difficult to please, and we've known the frustration of trying to live up to their expectations. If we can't please some people on this planet, can you imagine how tough it must be to please God? But God's response is wonderfully encouraging. I would think that He would have responded with a long list of rather intricate things to do and not to do. But instead He responded with a short list of the things that He requires. Three, in fact. The prophet Micah declared, "He has told you, O man, what is good; and what does the Lord require of you but to do justice, to love kindness, and to walk humbly with your God?" (v. 8). The phrase "to love kindness" means to be passionately addicted to mercy. There are some things that I am passionately addicted to in my life: Martie, my children, pasta, a few good friends, and NCAA college basketball March Madness. God calls me to be passionately addicted to compassion. His kind of compassion.

43

I think we need to remind ourselves that compassion is a response —a constructive, caring, remedial response to real needs, regardless of who has the need. We respond to needs in a variety of ways. Some of us are quick to be *judgmental*, seeking to analyze why the problem is there in the first place. When we find a mistake in action or attitude, we judge the one with the need for getting himself in the fix he's in. Others respond with *apathy*, seemingly numb to the pain of another's predicament. Some of us respond with *curiosity*, like Sherlock Holmes, delving through every detail to satisfy our curiosity without much thought of reaching out to help. Others, to their credit, respond with *sympathy* and sometimes *empathy*. They are touched with the problem and feel for the person. But the last and authentically biblical response is the response of *compassion*.

Compassion Defined

What is true biblical compassion? Several words are used in Scripture to translate our English word "compassion." Their meanings in both Hebrew and Greek are highly instructive. There are two basic words in the Old Testament, one of which means "to bear, to become responsible for, to spare someone from trouble." Whereas the first word deals mainly with our actions, the second is more attitudinal. It means "to be soft, gentle." The word is sometimes translated "womb," and it also means to "be wide" in terms of encompassing others and their needs. In the New Testament, the leading word for compassion means "that emotion aroused by contact with affliction." It is the Greek word used to translate the Old Testament concept of God's loyal, unfailing, covenant love. The stress in this particular word is on the action that flows out of our being as we are touched by another's affliction. In fact, the difference between sympathy and biblical compassion is that biblical compassion, true compassion, always leads to action. Compassion is not measured by how I feel, but rather by what I do in response to how I feel.

We might define compassion as *our commitment to activate ourselves as channels of God's love, mercy, and grace in tender, thoughtful, understanding acts of help, deliverance, forgiveness, and restoration toward those in need.* Compassion really is God's love, mercy, and grace looking for a place to get busy. Compassion asks, "What can I do to help?"

God's compassion is consistent. It is what He does in the season that stretches out before He ultimately must judge sin. His compassion never takes sin lightly or discounts His sense of justice. The story of the prodigal son made that clear. Christ's presence at the core of the crowd with the worst kind of people of His day did not mean that He didn't understand the depth and offense of sin. What He did understand, though, was that in spite of the great weight of sin, God valued the worth of the sinner. God's compassion is His consistent response, a season of grace and mercy, from a God who is "not wishing for any to perish but for all to come to repentance" (2 Peter 3:9).

Our problem is not that we are unable to activate compassion, but rather that our compassion is so inconsistent and selective. The inconsistency of our compassion is apparent as we measure it with real events in life. How would you respond if you were to hear that:

(1) a typhoon has devastated Malaysia;
(2) a major plane crash has killed hundreds in Detroit;
(3) an AIDS victim who lives in your town has died, and, your newspaper relates, he was a leader in the gay rights movement;
(4) a dog in your neighborhood has been hit by a car;
(5) a convict was shot while escaping;

(6) a family of another color on your street has been receiving threatening phone calls;

(7) a tragedy has struck someone who has misused and deeply offended you;

(8) homeless persons are begging money on the street where you work;

(9) the abortion doctor in your town discovered a bomb planted in his new 600-series Mercedes Benz as he was about to leave for the airport to spend the weekend at his condo in Palm Springs?

Well, how did you score? What would your attitudes, reactions, and actions have been in each case? It would be safe to say that in each of the cases above God would search for the mercy and grace realities that would dictate the kind of action that should be taken in the light of both truth and eternity.

Barriers

Why is it that we tend to deny His character through our lives by being so selective in our compassion reactions? Several reasons are reflected in Scripture. First and perhaps foremost is the barrier of our propensity to *prejudice*. In John 4, Jesus Christ did something that not one of His disciples would have done. Not because they weren't religious or weren't committed to Christ; just simply because their culture had cultivated within them a prejudice that would have neutralized their capacity to extend compassion. While they went into town to buy dinner, Christ sat, exhausted after a long day of ministry, by a well in Samaria. As the story goes, a woman came for water. Christ immediately was moved to compassion.

A multitude of prejudicial barriers would have gotten in the way of any one of us ordinary folk. First of all, she was a Samaritan, so there was an ethnic barrier. Jews had nothing to do with Samaritans. Second, she was a woman, and no Jewish rabbi would permit himself to have anything to do publicly with a woman, let alone a woman of Samaria. Third, Christ already knew that she was a woman whose lifestyle was less than admirable. She was working on her sixth husband. Should a rabbi who says that He is God in the flesh really be caught talking to a Samaritan woman who sleeps around the town? Christ leapt the barriers of prejudice, saw the need in her heart, and compassionately focused the gospel to meet her right where she was. We too are saddled with a multitude of cultural prejudices—prejudicial barriers of class, gender, race, region, and status. Prejudices against certain lifestyles and behaviors, making it nearly impossible for us to separate the sin from the worth of the sinner. Unless we, like Christ, are willing to repent of our prejudice, we too will stand compassionless at the fringe of the crowd with the self-righteous religionists of our day who wouldn't think of extending the mercy of God to people like these . . . like these tax-gatherers and sinners.

Perhaps our barrier to compassion is our sense of *inadequacy*. In John 6 Jesus Christ is faced with a crowd of 5,000 men plus their wives and children who have been with Him all day, and now that it is dinner time they have nothing to eat. How would He react to this massive physical need that surrounded Him on the hillsides? Interestingly, He tested His disciples by asking them where they could get enough money or food to feed a crowd like this. Philip responded that there wasn't nearly enough money in the treasury, and Andrew found a boy who had brown-bagged it to the revival service. But, as Andrew said upon presenting the lunch to Christ, "What are these among so many?" Just two small fish and five meager loaves. There will be times that the needs around us seem overwhelming, and in the face of them we will feel inadequate. But that is not the time to walk away. This little boy gave all he had. Although it wasn't much, it was all that he had, and food to a boy is a precious thing. But that little became much in the hands of the Master.

Your "little" may be a ministry of prayer. A small gift given at an appropriate time. A smile. A handshake. A hug. Or just an assuring glance.

One of the most difficult assignments I've ever had in the ministry was to break the news to the wife of a godly missions executive that on a missions trip to Alaska his plane had gone down in the ocean, and he was feared dead. In time the worst became the reality, as indeed he had died in that plane crash. This all happened on the verge of his retirement, when his widow would have finally had her husband as her own in the final days of their lives. But now, just when that gift from God would be hers, God snatched him away. Her pain was deep and her struggle enormous. I'll never forget the Sunday that she came to me and said she had just been wonderfully ministered to. I asked her what she meant. She said many people had told her that God was too wise to make a mistake and too good to be unkind, and that all things would work together for good. She said, "I know those things, but somehow they never brought comfort to my heart. But today in the church foyer, Pastor, someone walked up to me, put their arms around me, held me, and never said a thing." She went on to say, "It was like the arms of God around my life." It wasn't much, but it was a lot.

Street Barriers

Sometimes we may feel inadequately prepared to express compassion to someone who is offensive to us in terms of our Christian values. How do we express concern and compassion for the souls of those who are caught in the sin of homosexual lifestyles, who promote abortion on demand, or who pass out condoms in the schools our children attend? We can train our hearts to pray for them, that God would bring some influence into their lives to let them know of their sin and help them to focus on their Savior. And we can also pray that the Christians around them would deliver a truly compassionate witness.

Not everybody will be called or enabled to be front-line people on the streets of our urban centers, where the despair and the needs are so great. But many are already there, stunning neighborhoods with the grace of God, waiting for people like us to bring *robes*, *rings*, and *shoes* for those who are repenting on the streets of our city. We can be those who resource, the middle men who are actively busy about compassion transactions with people we could never possibly relate to.

The church today is blessed with a myriad of both churches and Christian organizations that have ministries to AIDS patients, homosexuals, street people, gang members, the homeless, the poor, the disadvantaged and physically disabled. Crisis pregnancy centers and adoption agencies are compassion alternatives to abortion. City ministries continue to effectively reach the needy for Christ. If you can't be a front-liner, you can always be a partner. And no gift, no prayer, no volunteer time is so small that it's inadequate.

If for some reason prejudice and inadequacy don't hinder us, some of us will no doubt be stymied by the barrier of *curiosity*. I find it instructive that in John 9, as Christ is walking into a city, a beggar born blind catches the attention of the disciples. Instead of responding with compassion, they succumb to curiosity—in fact, what makes their curiosity more respectable is that it is a theological curiosity. They ask Christ, "'Rabbi, who sinned, this man or his parents, that he should be born blind?' Jesus answered, 'It was neither that this man sinned, nor his parents; but it was in order that the works of God might be displayed in him.'" Then Jesus made clay and applied the clay to the man's eyes and said, "Go, wash in the pool of Siloam." The man went, washed, and saw. Important to note, isn't it, that the work of God that was to be displayed through his life was a work of compassion? A work that got busy about meeting the real needs of a poor beggar. How easy it is for us to be caught up in a web of curiosity and forget the pain and the needs of the one caught in the situation that so intrigues us. We seem to love delving into the details of the dilemma more than we love seeking how we can perform acts of deliverance on one's behalf.

I can't help but wonder if, when those disciples passed by the beggar born blind, they hadn't become *numb* to his presence there. They no doubt had walked by him on many occasions. We have a way of growing accustomed to other people's pain. Those in media don't help, as they carry us via satellite to tragic events around the world. We see the pain, the blood, the agony and, for three minutes, hear a detailed account. Then we're back to the studios where a smiling anchor person says, "And now this . . ." as an animated bunny rabbit bangs its drum across the screen. Tragedy has a way of becoming distant and unreal, and our culture has a way of anesthetizing us to the pain and problem of it all.

Luke 10 demonstrates that our propensity to be discompassionate may be caused by our *busyness*, *pride*, or *position*. In Luke 10 the disciples ask Christ what it means to love your neighbor. He told the parable of the Good Samaritan which relates the tragic story of a man beaten by thieves and left to die in the ditch. The "good people" of this world—people of power and position—pass by, ignoring his plight, no doubt because of their busyness or perhaps the exalted positions of their places in society. Christ then related that a Samaritan traveler reached out and sacrificed his own resources to meet the need of his enemy who had been victimized by thieves.

Luke 15 indicates that it's possible for *poor theology* to stand in the way of a compassion transaction. Wasn't that exactly why the Pharisees were so distraught that Jesus Christ would care for the very people they saw as the enemies? The people they were so angry about? The people who callously and carelessly contradicted all that the Jews held to be of value and worth? The Pharisees had what I call a "Good guys, Bad guys" theology. Since God is a holy, perfect, and good God, His favor must inevitably rest on those who were good and not deserving of His judgment. To those who were bad and deserving of His judgment, the only thing that God would have would be disfavor and condemnation. That's precisely why Jesus Christ was such an enigma to them. How could someone who came and claimed to be God spend time with prostitutes, tax collectors, and others who were the despised elements of Jewish society? If He were really God, He'd hang around with the good guys and from their side of the line pronounce clear condemnation on the bad guys. And while they were right about God's holiness and justice, there was something dreadfully lacking in their theology. And it was that their God was also a God of mercy, grace, patience, forbearance, and love. They had forgotten David's claim in Psalm 145:8–9 where the king wrote, "The Lord is gracious and merciful; slow to anger and great in lovingkindness. The Lord is good to all, and His mercies are over all His works."

Our theology, though orthodox to the core, can, if we are not careful, become distorted and misapplied. When that happens, life and, in this instance, compassion, get distorted as well. The sovereignty of God and the doctrine of election when not held in clear biblical balance can cool our hearts toward the lost and give us the distinct impression that if they will be saved, then God will get the work done if He wants to. A theology infected with temporalism could lead one to think that God has commissioned the church to save America, when a true understanding of biblical theology is that we are here not primarily to save America but to save Americans as well as non-Americans whose eternities are at risk.

Compassion Transactions

All of this is not to say that we shouldn't care about the demise of our culture and the rise of secular paganism around us. As we have noted, there would be something wrong with us if we did not feel the press of the deepening decadence. God expects us to do our best to hold our culture accountable for righteousness and to communicate the truth without intimidation. But as Paul wrote of the church that had reached maturity, it would be a church that would be characterized by "speaking the truth in love . . ." (Ephesians 4:15). Our culture must know us as truth-tellers, as truth-tellers with tears running down our cheeks if necessary both for those who perpetrate and those who are victimized by the ravages of sin.

As I drove to church one Sunday morning my attention became riveted to a report that was unfolding on the morning news. Late the night before, a church bus full of exhausted teenagers who had spent the day at King's Island amusement park came to the top of a rise in the road only to encounter the glaring headlights of an oncoming pickup truck. The head-on collision left the bus in flames, and that night many of those kids were entombed in the inferno of the bus. My instinctive response was one of heartbroken anger on behalf of the parents and families of those kids. I found myself focusing on the driver of that pickup truck, wondering why he'd be driving on the wrong side of an interstate. I thought to myself, "I bet he was drunk."

I was touched deeply, probably because I had on so many occasions been a parent waiting in the church parking lot for the ever-late buses to return. I reflected on all the times my kids stumbled off the bus and slumped into the seat next to me after a long day of fun with their friends. I found myself thinking about those parents who waited that night in the church parking lot, who, as the night wore on, wondered why the bus was so late, only to finally hear that the bus would never arrive and neither would their children.

I thought to myself, "If the driver was drunk, I hope they throw the book at him." And sure enough, later that day, the news carried the fact that the driver of the pickup truck had been drunk. Again my heart response was, "What a waste. I hope there's a good prosecutor in that northern Kentucky county." Later, a sense of biblical sanity began to work on my discompassionate, angry perspective. I was reminded that that truck driver had an eternity to face—that Christ had died for him, to deliver him even from the heinous, careless act of that Saturday night. It hadn't crossed my mind to pray for him, to pray that someone would get to him with the liberating message of Jesus Christ who came that all mankind, even the worst of us, might know His gracious liberation from judgment and be guaranteed the inheritance of heaven.

Dan Rather was on our campus some time ago to do an interview with our radio people on our coast-to-coast "Open Line" program regarding his new book and also what we supposed to be an anti-Christian bias in the media.[4] I have to admit that I had lumped Rather into the whole lot of media journalists who, it seemed to me, were committed to left-wing agendas that offended my sense of rightness and cultural, as well as historical, propriety. Whether that perception is warranted or not, it would be fair to say that some of these media types have never been my favorite kind of people. A friend of mine has a rubber brick that he throws at the TV set every time he's upset with an editorializing news journalist who is supposed to be reporting something of fact and instead is couching it in his own opinion and perspective. Well, I've felt like throwing that brick on more than one occasion.

When it came to Dan Rather, I was in for a big surprise in a lot of ways. We spent some time together during a break in the interview, and being in the middle of a whole litany of dramatic world-changing news stories like the fall of the Berlin Wall and the Persian Gulf war, I asked him if he had ever seen a year when there were so many radically profound news stories to cover. He said that there had never been a year in his career so full of important headlines.

He went on to say, "Now, I don't want to be a name-dropper, but several years ago I was talking with Billy Graham and I told him that the Communists had succeeded in obliterating religion. Graham replied, 'They haven't obliterated religion; they've only oppressed it.'" Rather went on to say, "I have to admit that Graham was right. I am shocked at the religious interest that has come to the surface in people's lives in the former Soviet Union and the Eastern bloc." As we chatted about this, I mentioned to him that the reason a person's interest in God cannot be obliterated is that man is built for a relationship with God. And although a particular person may not have a relationship with God or may even deny God's existence, the intrinsic longing for God cannot be erased from our souls.

I had already been surprised by how warm, open, thoughtful, and caring Dan Rather seemed to be. But my biggest surprise was yet to come. As we talked about man's need for God, he said, "Yes, I know, I grew up in a Baptist home." He went on to say, "In my grandmother's house, the only thing there was to read was the Sears Catalog and the Bible. And my grandmother read the Bible to me every day."

At the close of the interview, as our program host was discussing the issues of eternity, heaven, and hell with him, our host said, "Mr. Rather, I don't want to hurry anything, but if you were to die today and stand before God and God would ask you why He should let you into His heaven, what would you say?"

I thought that was a pretty bold way to end the interview and was very interested in Mr. Rather's response.

Since Mr. Rather is a professional accustomed to interviews, I knew that he could probably dance around that question and we wouldn't even have known when he was done that he had avoided it. But instead he met it head on and responded, "Well, it would be nothing of what I have done. It would have to be totally by the grace of God."

That's not what I had expected to hear.

As I watched the close of the Democratic convention that next summer with the balloons rising in the background and the confetti falling, Dan Rather and his co-anchor were drawing their coverage of the convention to a close and Rather said, "Well, if by the grace of God we're here four years from now, we'll do this again."

All of this to say that I know nothing really of Mr. Rather's personal commitment to Jesus Christ or what his spiritual condition is. The point is, and I say this to my shame, I had become so engulfed in temporal agendas that my responses to Dan Rather had always been within the context of politics and cultural perspectives. Why had I never thought of caring for him as a person, of caring for his soul, of praying that what no doubt were the prayers of a godly grandmother would finally come home in his heart?

I wonder when I'll learn to run down the path with God, taking the initiative with a heart of compassion, responding from an eternal perspective to those who need to be stunned by the grace of God through my life?

"Thou, O Lord, art a God merciful and gracious, slow to anger and abundant in lovingkindness and truth."
Psalm 86:15

"And so, as those who have been chosen of God, holy and beloved, put on a heart of compassion . . ."
Colossians 3:12

NOTES

1. Bob Davies, "Homosexuals and the Church: Will We Offer Hope?" *Moody* magazine, May 1994, 12–19.

2. Kenneth L. Woodward, John Barnes, and Laurie Lisle, *Newsweek*, "Born Again! The Year of the Evangelicals," October 25, 1976.

3. See also Romans 12:17–22.

4. This conversation took place in November of 1991 and is used with Mr. Rather's permission.

Moody Press, a ministry of the Moody Bible
Institute, is designed for education, evangelization,
and edification. If we may assist you in knowing
more about Christ and the Christian life,
please write us without obligation:
Moody Press, c/o MLM, Chicago, Illinois 60610.